KIDS IN CHINA

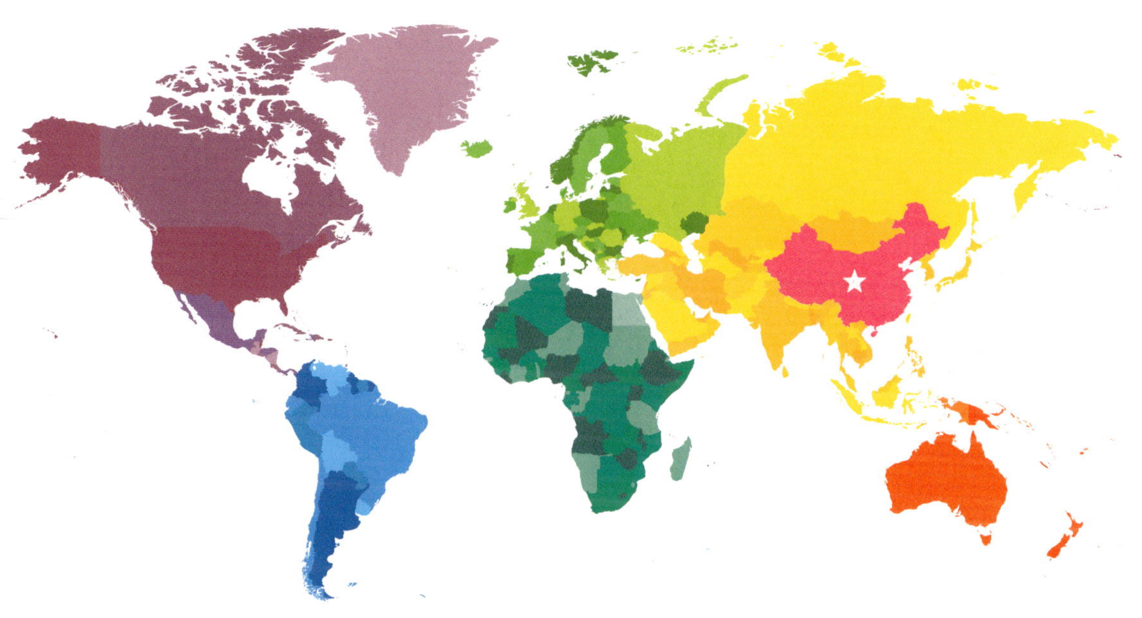

by Nikki Potts Ferguson

PEBBLE
a capstone imprint

Published by Pebble, an imprint of Capstone
1710 Roe Crest Drive, North Mankato, Minnesota 56003
capstonepub.com

Library of Congress Cataloging-in-Publication Data is available on the Library of Congress website.

ISBN: 9798875247804 (hardcover)
ISBN: 9798875247750 (paperback)
ISBN: 9798875247767 (ebook PDF)

Summary: Beautiful photographs and easy-to-understand text describe China's landmarks, festivals, sports, foods, transportation, and more.

Editorial Credits
Editor: Erika L. Shores; Designer: Sarah Bennett; Media Researcher: RebekahHubstenberger; Production Specialist: Tori Abraham

Image Credits
Alamy: Imago, 24; Getty Images: BJI/Blue Jean Images, cover (bottom), FangXiaNuo, 20, huoguangliang, cover (top), Lane Oatey/Blue Jean Images, 7, 18, 21, real444, 12, VCG, 13, 23, 27, 28, View Stock, 9; Shutterstock: astudio, 5, bonchan, 19, chinahbzyg, 11, 15, GuoZhongHua, 6, James Bronze, 16, Jojo Textures (rainbow border), cover and throughout, la.la.land, cover (globe icon), livebear chen, 25, MaraZe, 17, Pyty, back cover, 1, 4, T. Lesia, 29

Capstone thanks Frank Cai, Princeton, NJ, for his assistance in creating this book.

Printed and bound in Malaysia. 006460

TABLE OF CONTENTS

Words in **bold** are in the glossary.

WELCOME TO CHINA

Where is China? It is a large country in eastern Asia. It has mountains, deserts, and forests. Mount Everest is on China's border. It is the tallest mountain in the world.

Where in the world is China?

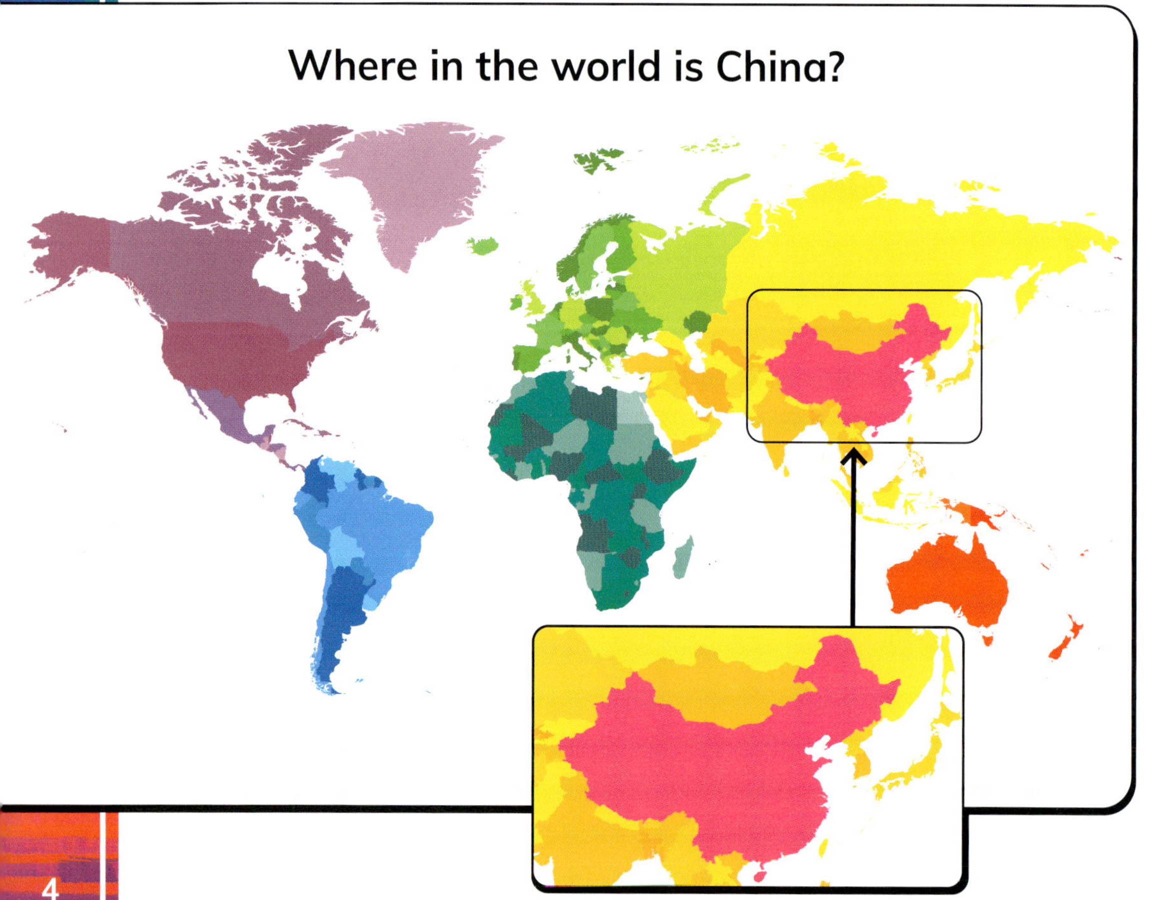

China is the second most populated country in the world. More than 1.4 billion people live there! What is life like for kids living in China?

AT HOME

Most people in China live in cities in the east. Many live in apartments. Some live in houses. Other people live in houses in **rural** areas.

Kids in China live with their parents and siblings. Their grandparents may also live with them.

TRAVEL AND SCHOOL

Students in China might walk to school. Many kids take the bus. Parents might drive them to school. Some kids ride bikes.

The school year in China is from September to July. Many schools in China require **uniforms**. Students might wear white shirts and sweaters. Girls might wear skirts. Boys might wear **trousers**.

Kids in China start primary school at age 6 or 7. Students spend time learning Mandarin Chinese, science, and math. They also learn about music and art.

At age 12, kids start junior secondary school. At age 15, students may go to senior secondary school. They might also choose to go to **vocational school**.

耕耘于分秒 收获于
社会主义核心价值观
24品格

FUN AND GAMES

Many kids in China enjoy paper cutting crafts. They might also go to waterparks or puppet shows. Families may visit **historic** sites like the Great Wall of China.

Soccer, basketball, and volleyball are played by kids in China. Others might participate in gymnastics or swimming. Forms of **martial arts** such as tai chi are also popular.

The most popular sport in China is table tennis. Two players stand on opposite ends of a table. A short net goes across the table.

Players hit a small ball back and forth with paddles. If a player hits the ball off the table or into the net, the other person gets a point. If a player can't hit the ball back over the net the other person gets a point. The first person to 11 points wins.

FOOD IN CHINA

Hard candies, shaved ice, and dried plum candy are popular in China. Kids also eat dragon's beard candy. This is made of sweet stringy strands that are wrapped around peanuts. When it was first created, the emperor thought it looked like a dragon's beard.

dragon's beard

Bubble milk tea is a favorite drink. Thick foam sits on top of milk and tea. Tapioca balls sit on the bottom.

Meats like duck, chicken, and pork are eaten often in China. Dumplings are small, shaped pieces of dough. They are filled with vegetables or meat.

chow mein

Chow mein is also popular. It is made of fried noodles. Meat, eggs, and vegetables are often added. Sauces are often mixed into chow mein.

LET'S CELEBRATE!

Chinese New Year is also called Spring Festival. It begins on the day the new moon occurs between January 21 and February 20. Families gather. They exchange red envelopes. The cards might have blessings written on them. Kids get money in their envelopes.

People watch fireworks. People decorate with red for luck. They hope for good luck in the upcoming year.

Dragon Boat Festival usually takes place in June. Some legends say it honors a popular leader from ancient China. Today, people watch dragon boat races. Long boats are decorated to look like dragons. People often eat rice dumplings during this holiday.

2 2

The Mid-Autumn Festival is celebrated between September and October. It is also called the Moon Festival. It is a **harvest** celebration. Families gather and pray. They are thankful for the harvest and good fortune.

Children hold paper lanterns.

mooncakes

People carry paper lanterns. They might release them into the sky. Mooncakes are often eaten during this holiday. People might give them to friends.

The Lantern Festival celebrates the first full moon of the new **lunar** year. It usually happens in February. Kids and families decorate lanterns. They use them to decorate their homes. People write **riddles** on their lanterns for people to solve.

Families dance and watch fireworks. They might go to a parade. Sweet rice balls are a popular treat.

China has more than 4,000 years of history. People of all ages enjoy living in and visiting the country. Mooncakes, table tennis, and festivals await in China!

FAST FACTS

Location: Eastern Asia

Capital: Beijing

Population: 1,416,043,270 people

Size: 3.7 million square miles
(9.6 million square kilometers)

Official Language: Mandarin Chinese

Currency: Yuan

GLOSSARY

harvest (HAR-vist)—to collect or gather crops that are ripe

historic (HISS-tor-ik)—having to do with events that happened in the past

lunar (LOO-nur)—having to do with the moon

martial arts (MAR-shuhl ARTS)—ancient Chinese methods for fighting or defending oneself

riddle (RID-uhl)—a statement or question that makes you think and that often has a surprising answer

rural (RUR-uhl)—having to do with the countryside

trousers (TRAW-surs)—a pair of cloth pants

uniform (YOON-uh-form)—special clothes that members of a group wear

vocational school (voh-KAY-shuhn-ul SKOOL)—a school that trains students for a job

READ MORE

Hustad, Douglas. *Your Passport to China.* North Mankato, MN: Capstone, 2021.

Layton, Christine. *Travel to China.* Minneapolis: Lerner, 2022.

Yim, Natasha. *Lunar New Year.* Minneapolis: Jump! Inc., 2024.

INTERNET SITES

Britannica Kids: China
kids.britannica.com/kids/article/China/345666

Globe Trottin' Kids: China
globetrottinkids.com/countries/china

National Geographic Kids: China
kids.nationalgeographic.com/geography/countries/article/china

INDEX

ABOUT THE AUTHOR

Nikki Potts Ferguson is a children's author and editor. Besides writing, she enjoys reading, crafting, and spending time with her family. Nikki lives in Kentucky with her husband, daughter, two cats, and dog.